HOME IN BLOOM

LESSONS FOR CREATING FLORAL BEAUTY IN EVERY ROOM

ARIELLA CHEZAR

WITH JULIE MICHAELS

PHOTOGRAPHY BY GENTL & HYERS

TEN SPEED PRESS
California | New York

To my children: August Oak & Celeste Neva

A WALK ON
THE WILD SIDE

With each chapter, I stray a little further into the meadow.

have always been fascinated by the magic of flowers. No matter the season, no matter the style of home, bring a bouquet of flowers into a room and the space is transformed. The life force inherent in a handful of blossoms or an abundantly flowering branch is the same: Both lift the space by adding color, scent, texture, and drama.

My goal has been to visit the homes of friends and acquaintances, mostly in the New England region where I live, and elevate the experience by adding flowers. Some spaces hold simple arrangements; in others, I take a deep dive into fantasy by exploring, for example, what a bathtub might look like surrounded by wild roses. I also wander further afield, visiting a New York City loft and a colonial villa in Merida, Mexico.

Whatever the location, I prefer to use flowers true to their season and environment. Tulips and dahlias fill the vases of a New England farmhouse, while bougainvilleas overflow in the Mexican villa. I take my inspiration from the colors of a room and also from its design: Is it modest and casual, welcoming friends around a country dining table? Or is it ornate and dramatic, calling for a more elaborate presentation?

In arranging my chapters, I've chosen certain rooms and situations that inspire the addition of flowers. "Welcome," for example, shows the flowers that might grace an entrance and invite a visitor indoors. "Nourish" refers to the rooms that feed us, either for dining or for restoring our souls. "Celebrate" takes those spaces to another level, when a special event is worthy of a spectacular table setting or an arrangement that captures the drama of the moment. "Pause" addresses our more individual spaces: a bedroom side table boasting flowers that echo a comfortable pillow, a quiet corner with a perfect reading chair. The "Wilding" chapter breaks with more traditional designs and takes flower arranging on a more exotic turn, especially when photographed in the ruins of a Hudson River mansion.

Since I began my career as an eighteen-year-old selling Christmas wreaths on the sidewalks of New York, I have moved into and about

the world of flowers—from New England to New York to California and back home again to this tiny village in the Berkshires.

I have followed the fashion and, at times, created my own. In New York I was assistant to a designer who favored tight, controlled flower arrangements that, as I look back now, seemed to strangle the very blossoms he was celebrating.

In San Francisco, I was astonished by jasmine vines cascading through empty lots; there were floral gifts on every corner. To the eyes of a girl from winter-tossed New England, this western coast was filled with abundance. When hired to create flower arrangements for an Oakland restaurant, I gathered armloads of blossoms, filling huge marble urns with cascading roses, arching spirea, twining clematis, and fruit-laden branches. This became my signature style. I wanted each arrangement to look fresh-picked from the garden, fruit tumbling across tablecloths, colors building tone upon tone, like mini-rainbows of a single hue.

Now, back home in the Berkshires, I walk my three rescue dogs—all Great Pyrenees in shades of beige and white—and stand astonished in autumn fields of golden grasses. Wild asters bloom along the border, viburnums are rusting from red to brown. I feel undone by nature.

I have always incorporated wild elements into my arrangements, be they weeds, branches, or vines rich with berries. However, in recent years, those elements have become more compelling than some cultivated flowers. Don't get me wrong; a dahlia in full bloom still takes my breath away, as does a peony bursting in shades of coral and pink. But I don't feel the same about hothouse roses or a Gerbera daisy.

If I were to propose my own theory of floral design, it would echo the views of Shane Connolly, floral designer for the coronation of King Charles III. "We need to see ourselves simply as servants and ambassadors of nature," Shane wrote to his fellow designers. "You don't have to abandon your own unique style. All you have to do is abandon the idea that you are more important than nature, and that you need somehow to subdue and control it."

That's what I hope you'll see in the flower arrangements collected in this book. I find myself relying more and more on wilder elements, not the always-magnificent flowers ordered from specialized nurseries. Those cultivated flowers remain the showstoppers in my work, but it's the grasses and weeds I glean from local fields that give my arrangements a sense of place and a more natural style.

I learned this lesson most emphatically several years ago, when I joined Shane and two other outstanding floral designers—Emily Thompson and Christian Tortu—for a flower workshop in the south of France. We had gathered with our students at a three-star Michelin restaurant and inn near the Spanish border.

It was mid-July, and the blossoms we had ordered from the Paris flower market seemed too formal and unyielding when contrasted with the abundance of the countryside. We decided to put those buckets aside and take our class into the fields, where we foraged for plant material on the property, harvesting ferns and lichen-covered branches, wild clematis, and grapes ripe on the vine. Next we headed for the local market, where we sourced fresh herbs, fruits, and vegetables. All of these went into copper vessels requisitioned from the celebrated kitchen, each pot brimming over with an abundance of weeds and wildflowers.

I still thrill to the memory of that weekend, and now that I live in the country I have access to a wilder style of floral design. In the pages that follow, you'll see that even the most formal of my arrangements have something of the country tucked into their containers. I have even developed a fondness for the invasive wild rose that forms hedgerows on my farm, and the Queen Anne's lace that populates summer fields. With each chapter, I stray just a little bit further into the meadow, until I arrive at a crumbling Hudson River manse that inspires a full-tilt fantasy of nature's conquest.

I urge you to thumb through these pages and then walk in your own woods or fields or city park and find inspiration not in the perfect blossom but in the nature that surrounds you.

WELCOME

My favorite
houses
welcome
guests with
flowers.

I grew up in a house where guests were always welcome. My mother was Dutch, so we often had friends visiting from the Netherlands. The conversation would ricochet between languages as guests passed homemade bread and jam, drank strong coffee, and shared fond memories.

I've maintained that tradition in my own family. I love having friends around my table; we cook together, play games, drink good wine, and talk late into the evening. Another tradition I've continued is my mother's love of flowers. Her devotion was part of her nationality: The Netherlands still supplies 40 percent of the world's flowers. I have never visited a Dutch home that didn't display a colorful bouquet somewhere in the house.

My favorite houses welcome guests with flowers—in the entryway, on a hall table, or in a cozy kitchen. The grandest gesture, and often the easiest, is to cut branches from a spring-blooming tree. The delicate blush of a magnolia branch, ceiling-tall and dancing in a round vase, brings drama to the corner of a porch. You could just as well harvest apple blossoms, lilacs, or viburnum flowers— all regulars in a New England garden. Place them in a window seat, on a hall table, or anywhere they don't block traffic. You will need a sizable vase for such displays, one that is heavy enough to hold such bounty.

In fall, you can achieve a similar effect by cutting branches of a copper beech, euonymous, or katsura. These dramatic branches need no added flowers. They impress by their size and the sheer power of a single shade.

Always work with the seasons. Even if you don't grow your own flowers, the blossoms most available will be those that are harvested locally. More to the point, whatever is blooming in your home should reflect the flowers blooming outside. I always think of spring as tulips and peonies, late summer as dahlias and chrysanthemums,

winter as evergreen and amaryllis. For filler flowers—the greenery or cuttings that finish an arrangement—look to the out-of-doors. Harvest milkweed seedpods, asparagus ferns, twining clematis, tiny asters. It's these small additions that add a sense of place to your bouquets.

Color is your first concern when choosing flowers for a room. Anything goes with neutral walls, but stronger colors require a shade that complements or contrasts. Blue walls provide a backdrop for pinks, reds, and rusts. Green walls work well with gold and yellow. Pastel walls invite softer colors to echo those quieter shades. You can match colors to furnishings—highlighting the tones in a throw pillow or sofa.

You can also find inspiration in a painting or other art piece. A blue, orange, and yellow wall hanging is reflected in my choices for a fireplace mantel filled with orange and yellow tulips. They are displayed at various heights, leading the eye up and down across the mantel. Blue vases make their own contribution to the drama, echoing the blue in the wall hanging.

Color is also paramount in combining flowers. I believe the best arrangements are created by building tone on tone. Choose one dominant color and then add variations by selecting similar shades for secondary blossoms. A hallway arrangement will draw the eye with rusty-red spider mums and peachy-pink dahlias. Add tall branches of euonymus, also called burning bush, which provides a dappled combination of both shades, and the whole suddenly becomes greater than its parts.

Whether you purchase flowers or grow your own, there is another reliable resource that is seasonally generous: the blossoms and greens that appear on the roadside or in abandoned fields. I have stopped my car to gather purple-blooming angelica or maidenhair ferns. Also available for roadside harvesting are wild roses or dried seedpods. All add drama to an arrangement and anchor it in its season.

THE RIGHT VASE

The right vase is just as important as the flowers that fill it. The magnolia branches (opposite) require a narrow-necked vessel that will hold them steady. This ceramic urn is heavy enough to nestle tall branches without tipping but is tapered at the mouth to keep them upright.

Over the years, I have collected several vessels that are in constant use for my larger arrangements. Two types, the curved compote (see page 44) and the stately urn (see page 38), work well with tall branches and abundant flowers, but both require preparation. The low, open style of the compote requires a spiky flower frog to hold stems in place. I then use green floral tape to create a lattice-like grid to further support the flowers. A tall urn might also require a taped grid into which you can better position flowers.

For smaller arrangements, like tulips (see page 63), think about using an "inverted triangle" vase, open-mouthed and tapering to a narrow *V*. Tulips are dancers—they arrive upright, but overnight begin to curve and curtsy. A wide-mouthed vase leaves them free to flow. By the same token, a tall, narrow vase emphasizes verticality and works well with one or two stems. Both styles are used on this tulip mantel.

'Holyhill Orange Ice' dahlias are the gift of a late-summer garden, especially when paired with cascading raspberry canes and 'Queen Lime' orange zinnias. The Queen Series zinnias are a newer variety and present wonderful variations in tone—starting with lime-green centers and spreading out into shades of orange, pink, or red. They are perfect for blending with other flowers. Note how I cluster the smaller zinnias deep into the arrangement. Even though dahlias steal the show, the zinnias hold their own.

Pale melon bougainvilleas and pink lisianthuses are paired with tropical foliage in this Mexican hallway, where they complement a magnificent tile floor. It was the mauve-pink walls that inspired this combination. Best to select older bracts of bougainvilleas, since newer blooms don't stay fresh in a vase.

A single peach-hued blossom set amid a grouping of white flowers and green tropical foliage links this tabletop arrangement to the colors and patterns in the spectacular tile floor.

The walls of this ruined Hudson River mansion inspired a palette of rust and green.'Honey Dijon' roses are clustered at the base, but it's the tall plume poppies and arching Solomon's seal that draw the eye upward. That height is balanced by branches of donut peaches and apples that curve down to the table.

I break the rules here, abandoning a focal flower and opting instead for a cloud of white flutter flowers. These purple-throated *Abyssinian gladioli*, or acidantheras, curve like a swan's neck and contrast well with their swordlike foliage. They share the spotlight with lilac clematis, while cascading sweet autumn clematis wanders down the tall cabinet and draws the eye upward.

To echo the blowsy floral wallpaper in the room, this generous arrangement gathers 'Honey Dijon' roses, strawberry digitalis, dahlias, and apple and peach branches against a backdrop of raspberry canes and burgundy ninebark. When assembling an arrangement of this size, it helps to concentrate each addition into its own section: ninebark on one side, raspberries on the other, and 'Honey Dijon' roses at the center.

FLOWERS IN THE KITCHEN

Too often, we pick or purchase a bouquet, arrange it, and place it carefully in the living room or on the dining room table. But what about the kitchen? That's where families spend a large part of their day. I always have bud vases above my sink that display lilies of the valley, grape hyacinths, or whatever small blossoms are in season. You'll also find mason jars filled with mint, parsley, or lemon verbena—some gathered for cooking, others to steep for a calming cup of tea.

Think about breaking down that farmers' market bouquet; place some blossoms on a kitchen shelf, others in the bathroom. Sprinkle joy throughout the house.

This kitchen is decorated with four arrangements that share the golden orange color of spicy-smelling marigolds. A large champagne bucket elevates this humble flower by inviting it to tumble as if still in the garden. Smaller vases hold tiny tangerine gem marigolds, while creamsicle orange nasturtiums spill from a shelf.

The copper pots of this New York City loft inspire two dramatic arrangements dominated by assorted Itoh peonies. They are paired with the bell-like blossoms of the martagon lily and, in the larger arrangement, joined by Polkadot Series foxgloves and framed by the blooming burgundy branches of the physocarpus, or ninebark. Clematis vines balance all that height, but it's the peonies that dominate.

This smaller arrangement proves the power of one: that spectacular Itoh peony. Multiple branches of martagon lilies can barely hold their own.

Tulips in various shades of terra-cotta and peach, some tall and curving, others cut short and tight, are displayed on a mantel, forming an almost single arrangement. This is a demonstration of how the impact of one type of flower, linked by color and shape, can change by how you arrange it.

Here's an arrangement in which flowers are secondary to the foliage; in this case, the huge, gesturing branches of euonymus as it makes an autumn journey from pale green to bright burgundy. Nestled at the center are 'Cafe au Lait' dahlias and burgundy spider chrysanthemums, but it's the movement and form of the euonymus that makes the magic.

Sometimes I like to pair opposites on the color wheel, especially when I see how red nerine spider lilies pop against a blue wall. They're joined in this silver compote by shaded purple anemones that contrast in shape as well as color. Note how blue-patterned cups, each holding a single lily, extend the impact of a simple arrangement.

NOURISH

It doesn't
take much
to trigger joy.

Studies show that flowers not only brighten a room, they also lift your mood and boost creativity. A simple garden rose can delight with color and scent. Pause a little longer and observe its complex structure, surely a wonder of nature.

It doesn't take much to trigger joy. As a lover of peonies, a spring-summer blossom so majestic that one can stand alone in a vase, I often clip individual flowers to display on a bookshelf or in a bud vase above the sink. Instant pleasure.

Still, there are times you want to go with the WOW of a grand arrangement displayed on the dining room table. Think about building tone on tone, starting with a focal flower that dominates and sets the style. You may match it to a tablecloth or to your favorite dishware.

If you are entertaining in the late summer or early fall, draw on the abundance of nature. This is when you can augment arrangements with fruited boughs heavy with peaches or crabapples. Gather wild chokecherry from the roadside or add long raspberry canes, some still bearing green fruits. Often I grow flowers as much for their seedpods as for their blossoms—think opium poppies, alliums, or love-in-a-mist. All add playful texture to an arrangement.

A good recipe for larger displays follows the progression below.

Greens: These can be clipped from trees such as katsura or smoke bush, or gathered, such as with Solomon's seal or geranium foliage. They add texture and a sense of place.

Focal flower: The drama queen, usually a dominant blossom like a peony, dahlia, iris, or rose.

Filler flowers: Smaller blossoms that add texture, depth, and complementary colors. Sometimes these are clustered along a stem, like delphinium or foxglove.

Floater flowers: These small blossoms continue the color theme while floating over large arrangements. Think martagon lilies, stems of tiny orchids, or sweet peas.

Vines: Add vines to an arrangement and extend its impact, curling around a vase or skimming a tabletop. All manner of clematis vines will accomplish this feat.

For smaller bouquets, try limiting your choices to one or two blossoms. In several bathroom arrangements, I match or contrast a color palette. When orange and purple anemones share a vase (see page 72), their strong colors create a bold dynamic. In another smaller arrangement (see page 70), pale pink lisianthuses pair with a similar shade of Sheffield daisy. Here it's the contrast of shapes that draws the eye.

Sometimes less is more, as when you concentrate on a single blossom. You can arrange an abundance of single-species dahlias into a giant bouquet or gather lavender plectranthus in tiny vases to add soft colors to a bathroom. This works especially well when your flower garden explodes with late-summer flowers and you don't want to waste a single one.

FRUIT AS THE STAR

Late summer produces a cornucopia of fruits and vegetables so spectacular
that they can play a major role in an arrangement. Look closely at the bouquet
opposite and you will discover only a single blossom—a Labyrinth dahlia—
at the center of a table bouquet where fruit is the star. Most dominant are
branches of donut and regular peaches, as well as cascades of chokecherries.
The deep burgundy of smoke bush foliage complements the tiny cherries, even
as cephalanthus balls float above the grouping, adding an ethereal quality.

THE POWER OF ONE—OR TWO

The seven stems of fritillaria, opposite, are displayed in three tea glasses on various levels. They complement the painting of a lemon in the background and, by being displayed separately, make a stronger impression. This is often the way I display favorite flowers after a lap around my garden: I'm busy and don't have time to make anything fussy, but I am so drawn to the magic of these colors that I can't abandon them. Fill some glasses with water, position flowers artfully, and go about your business.

Here's a bucket of 'Peaches and Cream' and 'A la Mode' dahlias waiting to be featured in an arrangement (opposite). Note how they pick up background colors: the copper faucet, the wooden window frame, and, most important, the exquisite pattern on this homeowner's china. Every room holds hints as to what color combinations will work best. The choice of these flowers for this kitchen was a no-brainer.

This 'Julia Rose' Itoh peony is one of a new breed of "intersectional" peonies with magnificent single to semi-double blossoms that change color with time. Itohs are modern crosses between the familiar herbaceous peony and the more exotic tree peony. Now that it's displayed on this shelf, I can watch its journey from pink to pale.

What's my favorite flower in this arrangement? It's not the splendid garden rose, whose peachy hue establishes the theme. It's the 'Cherry Caramel' phlox, a smaller filler flower that invites us to celebrate its two-tone charm. This kind of blossom is a boon to floral designers as it adds depth to any arrangement. The purple echinops, or globe thistle, in the background quietly echoes the purple glassware on the table, a subtle but important connector.

home in bloom

DRAMATIC SETTINGS

How could any plant compete with the spectacular Mexican tiles that fill the shower room of this Merida home? Pull back (see pages 94 to 95), and you'll see how unusual the space really is: It's about the size of a small bedroom. If I were in New England, I'd fill this room with masses of lilacs or the limbs of a flowering crabapple. Here, I clip the branches of a Mexican fire bush, a common tropical shrub; its red blossoms are almost as dramatic as the floor.

This spring bouquet takes its inspiration from a painting that celebrates lavender and green. Fill a glass urn with a branch or two of magnolia, then visit your garden for complementary colors; in this case, a few upright narcissi and the ruffled edges of a violet 'Cummins' tulip. A pair of 'Pink Star' double tulips, which look a lot like peonies, demands attention.

GOING GREEN

In flower arranging, green often acts as a neutral, softening strong colors such as those in the fire flower, below. This remarkably tiled floor serves the same purpose. Though elaborate, the tile's green coloring balances these flowers.

A concrete planter makes sense in this expansive Mexican shower room, where tall branches of a Mexican fire bush pair with scads of green baby mangoes (opposite) growing on the vine. Bathrooms are a great location for potted plants and grand gestures; they both crave the moisture.

FLOWERS IN THE BATH

There is no better solace for a working mother than a hot bath at the
end of the day. I'll light a candle and add a simple grouping of flowers, just
to have something to admire while I bathe. There's no need for anything
complicated: Snip some stems from a potted plant or fill a vase with lilies
of the valley, picked for their fragrance. Garden roses are another aromatic
option. They can travel to another room once you've finished bathing.

A riot of 'Avignon Parrot' tulips light up a room. Orange is also dominant in the arrangement of bright ranunculus and purple hellebores on the page opposite. Note the tiny wood carving of the fox above the sink. Thence comes the inspiration.

Candlelight and garden roses that calm with their sweet scent fill this bathroom with fragrance.

CELEBRATE

Create a palette that reflects the season and the setting.

I am a working mother of two adolescents, three dogs, five cats, and a dozen hens. My life is a tight schedule of meetings, pickups, and music lessons. But give me a birthday, an anniversary, or a visit from my sister and I'll cook dinner for twenty. That's the pleasure of welcoming company. My favorite experience is a room full of people dining, laughing, and enjoying themselves.

Given my profession, I never entertain without flowers. But given my reality, I don't have time for complex arrangements at home. Usually the flowers that grace my table are clipped from whatever is blooming in my backyard: multiples of tulips, daffodils, or dahlias dancing down the table in tiny vases. And candles—always candles.

Fortunately, I can indulge my more elaborate entertaining fantasies in the flower workshops I host here in the Berkshires, and also in Amsterdam, Mexico, and Hawai'i. For these, my students might harvest their own flowers, visit the local flower market, and forage in the fields. We always finish with a dinner that highlights what they've learned, creating a palette that reflects the season and the setting.

These workshops afford the opportunity to experiment with color schemes I seldom use in my wedding designs, where brides have their own preferences. In my workshops, I might use a piece of fabric for inspiration, a colorful tile, even a patterned skirt purchased on Etsy. Combine this with seasonal flowers, match it to the setting, and you have liftoff.

Once, at a workshop in Maui, I shared an exotic piece of floral wallpaper with the class, excited by the combination of oranges and reds. A powder-blue background added a dramatic twist. We used those tones and a tropical motif to build a remarkable tablescape.

Before you launch any festive event, determine your inspiration point. Where are you? What season is it? What are the beautiful elements you want to feature and what are those colors? Sometimes the inspiration point can be a china pattern, a painting, a wall color. Sometimes it can be a flower.

Last spring, when I taught my workshop in Holland, I selected a magnificent burgundy-and-white tulip for our final dinner. Using that one spectacular shade as inspiration, we built our arrangements around it, including a china dinner plate with a similar tulip pattern and adding other flowers and candles in complementary colors.

A grand celebration calls for more than just a table setting. This is a time to cut whole branches, gathering them in large urns to fill the room with color. Pile platters with perfect fruit or scatter them among the tableware. Forage for moss-covered logs and pair them with wildly crenellated mushrooms (easily store-bought), bringing a forest right into the room. Fashion a chandelier of pinecones or, better yet, one of autumnal branches of American beech wound around a metal base.

Sometimes the simplest solutions are the most inspired. Go to the garden center, buy three shrubs that fit your color choices in either leaf or bloom, plant them in pots, and place them where they have the most impact. Once the party's over, move them into the garden or onto the front porch. Or gather branches of a flowering tree or shrub in full bloom—think dogwood, lilac, or, in the South, crape myrtle. A large urn filled with one species, in abundance, can lift the room to another level.

DESIGNING FOR A
DINNER PARTY

When planning a special dinner party, here are three questions you should ask yourself: Where are we? What season is it? What are the elements I want to feature and what are their colors? This banquet table in Merida (see pages 113–117 for details) gets its color theme from a fruit: the orange-fleshed mamay sapote. I discovered these at an outdoor market and was immediately inspired by how their bright orange flesh contrasted with the elongated black pit.

These were joined on the table by locally harvested lemons and oranges, as well as branches of young mangoes, whose petite green fruits stole my heart. I added candles inspired by the mamay colors, then found black beads and pots of peperomia to pick up the darker tones. If you think of setting a table in the same way as building a bouquet, you'll see how each element contributes to the whole.

The combination of leggy branches and browny-green
lisianthuses provides more texture to this busy table,
and surprises guests by being such an unusual pairing.

BREAKING THE RULES

When setting a table, I usually opt for arrangements that don't impede the line of sight between dinner guests. No one wants to talk over the heads of interfering plants. But here's a table setting that breaks those rules (for details, see page 122). This late-fall table in a New York City loft boasts burgundy spider mums, also called Fuji mums, that are the royalty of the genus. They are paired with shorter golden mums. Spider mums are often used in Ikebana, or Japanese flower arranging, which emphasizes simplicity, shape, and line. That these burgundy and gold flowers also echo the gold-red tones of the American beech branches that fill surrounding pots makes this a perfect palette.

Spider mums are raised for their height, with each branch de-budded of any horizontal competition. I can't resist letting them tower over the table. But note how the arrangements are airy and open, with few leaves left to block sight lines. That said, if dinner discourse gets unusually spirited, some of these small pin-frogged vases might be removed from the table and find refuge on a neighboring windowsill. Not a problem; the flowers can delight from a distance.

home in bloom

How delightful that burgundy spider mums
echo the china and glassware set on this table.
Yellowing corydalis leaves fill out the tiny vases
but never approach eye level, where the true
magic takes place.

This classic 'Heather James' chrysanthemum (opposite) offers a fine contrast, in color and shape, to the burgundy mums. Note that sight lines between diners are kept relatively clear.

There's no restriction on height when you are designing for a buffet table. Dramatic yellow beeswax candles will be interspersed among this almost botanical arrangement of narcissi, each tiny vase holding a single species; they are gathered together in the larger compote. I expect the flowers will be pushed back and candles lit when food comes to the table. But what a joyous welcome to a spring dinner.

This compote anchors a pin frog that holds the tall stems of various white narcissi with different trumpets of chartreuse, yellow, and apricot. They are cut to varying heights, so each is easily viewed.

It's not difficult to find inspiration for this table setting. Look to the miraculous tiled floors in this Merida home, reference the walls painted in soft blue, and you've got your color scheme. I chose blue candles and tiny blue bud vases to carry color onto the table. But it's the tropical foliage that adds grandeur and gives guests a sense of place. I decided the floral additions to this Mexican table setting should be neutral so as not to overwhelm the other, more dramatic elements.

Rough-hewn dishes and majolica centerpieces pick up the rustic quality of the dining table, echo the greenery, and complete the look.

This is the kind of table you lay when the garden is bursting with dahlias and your guests are arriving shortly. No time for fussing, but given this collection of beauties, there's no need. Bud vases, each filled with a single blossom or three, display a variety of dahlias in complementary tones, some blousy, some tightly wound. Guests will be transfixed by the variety.

MARRYING HIGH AND LOW

As a floral designer, I am a frequenter of flower markets. I drive my van down to the famous New York City markets on Twenty-Eighth Street and search for floral perfection: peonies in soft shades of cream and peach, 'Honey Dijon' roses that wander closer to caramel on the color wheel.

But that's not the only stop I make. En route to New York, I pull over to harvest wild *Angelica sylvestris*, which thrives in local swamps, grows six to eight feet in height, and boasts huge umbrella-like flowers. Arranged in a large urn (at left), accompanied by cascading branches of *Stephanandra incisa*, it more than stands up to those "pretty girls" at the table. I love these combinations of high and low; it's like wearing a T-shirt with a couture skirt. They feed my desire to go wild and surprise guests with common Cinderellas who have been brought to the ball.

My "princess" flowers: They include 'Border Charm' and 'Garden Treasure' Itoh peonies and 'Pastelegance', an herbaceous peony in shades of pale pink and cream. There are a few cuts of yellow perennial foxglove, and the almost-flowering greens of *Stephanandra incisa*.

Here's another example of high-low design: The peonies on this page and opposite are joined in their vases by wild roses, also culled from the New England roadside, and tiny florets of lady's bedstraw, a regular in fallow fields.

This buffet table, draped in acid yellow linen, shows the impact of gathering flowers in a single mass. Since it's late summer, I am determined to celebrate the peach 'Queen Lime' zinnias so abundant in the garden. Their tone-on-tone coloring sets the stage for similarly hued apples and donut peaches still on the bough. I add a vase of 'Honey Dijon' roses to balance those lovely yellow candles.

PINK GOES PUNK

The blue peeling paint in this Hudson River mansion provides a backdrop
of possibility. One could contrast a variety of colors against this blue, but
I like going loud, with bright pink and rose tones, to celebrate a young
friend's birthday. Here again the solution is simple: differing sizes of vases
of pink 'Yves Piaget' roses and a bevy of foxgloves in Arctic Fox Rose. Even
the desserts follow the color scheme.

This blue, depression glass cake stand blends with the tablecloth and wall, but it's the extraordinary sugar flower cake, by Marion Attal, that thrills the birthday girl.

All elements reinforce the color code: blue glasses,
pink candles, and a platter of macarons.

home in bloom

FUNGI GET FANCY

Mushrooms have been sprouting everywhere in the design world. I suspect this is a result of inspiring walks in the woods during Covid isolation. We've discovered the dramatic variety of these fungi and also their greater availability in supermarkets and through specialty growers, which is where I found these pink oyster and brown Chestnut mushrooms (opposite). Once I decided on the theme for this hunter green dining room, I foraged in a local forest, harvesting rotted logs ablaze in emerald green moss, tiny ferns, and rough, rusting leaves. I even found a few mushrooms.

A large silver tray holds these woodland treasures, arranged as if to reproduce the forest floor. When paired with branches of wild raspberry, the result is slightly primeval.

home in bloom

This collection of pink and yellow oyster mushrooms, joined with Chestnut mushrooms, rests on a moss-encrusted log and enhances the primeval mood of the room.

PAUSE

I believe
in "traveling
flowers."

For me, one of the great joys of arranging flowers is the small moments of meditation it brings into my life. As I work with fragile blossoms, my too-busy schedule fades and I am lost in a world of color, texture, and scent. It is a reverie I welcome. All my senses— touch, sight, smell—are captured by each sensuous blossom.

By connecting with flowers, we can all experience those moments of transcendence. According to a 2020 article in the *Journal of Environmental Psychology*, the experience of merely looking at a flower significantly lowers blood pressure and cortisol level. A second study found that patients staying in hospital rooms containing flowers experienced lower levels of anxiety and fatigue.

That's why it's so important to spread the good vibrations. In addition to that beautiful arrangement on your dinner table, don't forget the single tulip tucked into a bud vase above the sink or the scented bouquet of garden roses by your bed. We are all made calmer by this connection to nature.

That's why I believe in "traveling flowers." A birthday dinner might require a generous table arrangement, or a grouping of mock orange branches in your entry hall. Once the guests have gone, move the mock orange into the bedroom, where their nocturnal scent can lull you to sleep. Or deconstruct that bouquet the next day and carry a small vase to your home office when you go to pay your bills. Take flowers into a bathroom, fill the tub, light a candle, relax.

While cut flowers may be periodic visitors to a home, potted plants are full-time residents. My dining and living rooms face south, where a wall of windows takes our view far into the Berkshire hills. In winter, every table and windowsill boasts a flowerpot. I am particularly fond of begonias, because their leaves are even more beautiful than their flowers. Sometimes I'll clip a stem and slip it into a narrow jar to root, and soon I'll have a whole new plant. I have a tall citrus tree that spends winter in a sunny corner and summer on the back patio.

Then there are the flowering pots that make their way into my home, starting with the crate of amaryllis I order each year from Dutch growers. These are my standard holiday present, but I always save enough to sprinkle around the house as they mature. Close on their heels come the flowering bulbs: tulips, hyacinth, and daffodils large and small. I grow some on my own, but they are all available at garden centers or the grocery store. I like to bunch small pots of these in groups of three—either on a windowsill or gathered into a favorite planter. Another winter distraction? Narcissus bulbs sunk into stones and lovingly watered. Set them in a glass vase on the kitchen table and watch, with awe, their daily progress.

Not all of us are fortunate enough to have a garden. But in whatever form it takes, scientists counsel that gardening is good for you. Digging in the soil reduces stress and heart disease, and provides exercise and a sense of community. Even a tiny garden means you can pick the salad greens for your dinner; the flowers you grow are an added gift. No matter how many exquisite flowers I order from domestic or overseas growers, a flower picked from my backyard is always my favorite.

The mauve pink walls in this Hudson, New York, house inspired an early autumn blast of pink and peach dahlias paired with smaller 'Profusion' zinnias. Note how, in the arrangement on the right, I display the zinnias in a sizable bunch so they can balance the larger flowers in the bouquet.

FLOWERS AS MEDITATION

Making a flower arrangement such as the one on the right is not much different from creating a painting. I have my paints (flowers); now I must balance color and shape to lead the eye through the arrangement. Where shall I add texture? How do I frame this picture? Such decisions require focus: Worldly demands fade, my vision narrows, and I am consumed with the trial and error of creativity.

Zinnias are the dominant flower here, ranging from light pink to peach and rose. Lisianthuses and dahlias fill out the frame, with the goal of balancing tone on tone interspersed with a few punchier moments. Raspberry canes add the green frame, and dry grasses punctuate.

If I have a palette I return to often, it's this one: peachy oranges, creamy whites, and plummy pinks. Here I combine three favorite dahlias: 'Peaches n' Cream', 'A la Mode', and 'Emory Paul' pink. They bloom at the same time that euonymus turns from green to shocking pink, making this a luscious combination.

This Dutch amaryllis, 'Rilona', is not one you'll find on supermarket shelves. The greater investment pays off in this unique color. Here, they complement tall blue vases and a dark blue wall that match them in intensity.

A combination of Itoh and herbaceous peonies appear here with pink poppies, wild and cultivated roses, lady's bedstraw, raspberry foliage, and the tiny pink blossoms of *Gillenia trifoliata*, or Bowman's root, which is native to the eastern United States. I love the way these soft pink punctuations float over the drama of the crowd.

These lavender and mauve garden roses rise from low to high in a narrow glass vase, demonstrating how a good pair of clippers can trim a flower into many heights, making a simple arrangement more dramatic.

AN ASIAN INFLUENCE

Peonies date back to 1000 BCE in China, where they dominated imperial flower gardens. Given the bold carpeting in this New York City loft, and the two Chinese horseshoe chairs—a style popular in the Song dynasty—I thought the room called for boldly colored peonies. These 'Nippon Beauty' single peonies with confetti centers pair well with orange martagon lilies, and the burgundy blooms of physocarpus hold their own in this colorful setting.

A close-up of peony, orange garden roses, lily, and physocarpus shows how each provides not only a different color but an entirely different profile, which makes this an electric arrangement.

An Eames chair seemed a good inspiration for this arrangement, especially when paired with this glorious Italian vase. The autumn season invited a combination of rudbeckia, 'Senior's Hope' dahlias, peach boughs, beet greens, plume poppy, and smoke bush foliage.

When water meets floating flower petals the effect
is meditative. Here, plumeria blossoms are scattered
dreamily in a garden swimming pool.

Nerine lilies show the impact of a single blossom. Variety comes from massing the flowers in vases of different heights.

DINNER PLATE DRAMA

Who can resist a pink wall? It inspires this punchy color palette, all shades of hot pink dahlias, some of the "dinner plate" variety. Add Elaeagnus branches to add height and draw the eye upward.

Here's an unusual combination—I wouldn't generally pair yellow and pinky-purple anemones. But look closely: These Japanese anemones have a yellow center. It seems just right to add a handful of yellow nasturtiums to the grouping, especially when they appear as a solid block to keep the contrast pronounced.

There are flowers, and then there are delphiniums—kings of the cottage garden. In a bedroom with dark green walls, they light up the space with no need for companions.

'Etched Salmon' and coral peonies
join wisps of clematis vine to
complement the soft salmon duvet.

OUT IN THE SUMMER AIR

A New England screened porch welcomes summer visitors with fragile greens that have wintered indoors. Each year, you can add to this collection of pots, filling some with annuals that will stay only a season, snipping back others that need a haircut, finding attractive pots for the plants bought at a local garden center. Begonias, geraniums, a fig tree—they make a jolly restful scene. Just hang a hammock and celebrate the season.

Crabapple boughs, green peaches, snowberries, and Queen Anne's lace invite a visitor to nap on this chaise. Note the crumply yellow foliage: branches of the unfamiliar white forsythia.

WILDING

There is
a way to
design that
embraces
the rough-
and-tumble.

It's the wilder bits of Mother Nature that have always attracted me. While growing up, my sister and I spent many hours playing outdoors, which gave me an appreciation for wandering vines, perky asters, and beech leaves turning copper in the sun. As it is with most children, my first bouquets were made of dandelions.

Don't get me wrong. I'm still brought to my knees by a special blossom: the pristine narcissus, glistening for just a few precious days. Or a ruffled parrot tulip, its crunchy petals pierced by a palette of bright colors. I adore flowers in every shape and form, but I often feel conflicted when I order ranunculus from a distant grower, given the fossil fuels used to deliver those beauties to my back door.

Perhaps that's why I recoil from designers who focus exclusively on imported flowers. I want to show people there is a way to design that embraces the rough-and-tumble, and is better for our struggling planet. It's this integration of the wilder elements that set my work apart thirty years ago, and it is the wilder elements that draw me still. The weeds so many of us ignore, or try to eradicate, play an integral role in our larger ecosystem. They are restoring the ground that we have overcultivated.

That's why I am so impressed by Isabella Tree, whose book *Wilding: The Return of Nature to a British Farm* describes how she and her naturalist husband let their 3,500-acre farm revert to wilderness.

Those acres now hold the nests of once-endangered nightingales; they have become a breeding ground for purple emperor butterflies and turtledoves. A stretch of the Adur River, returned to a shallow floodplain, now welcomes wildflowers, insects, and otters.

Making use of local flora, I collect wormwood, or Sweet Annie, in abandoned fields and along the roadside. I also clip bits of Queen Anne's lace, artemisia, and twisted blackberry vines. All of these make their way into some of my most formal arrangements.

home in bloom

In this chapter, I invite readers to step out of their everyday expectations of what flowers can be and enter a dreamscape where nature invades a room rather than inhabits it.

I have been fortunate to discover several locations with their own wild contributions. A beautifully tiled Mexican villa came with a garden exploding with plants that few of us see outside of a greenhouse. Here, I was drawn to tropical foliage, which I paired with generous bougainvillea. I wrapped abundant vines around dramatic bedposts.

The wood and fields surrounding a Hudson River studio are the perfect foil for another exploration of floral excess. I turn blooming knotweed into a hanging chandelier. (This is an invasive species that requires special treatment: All remnants went into garbage bags after the shoot and were delivered to the local dump.) Nearby, I located an old mansion that has seen better days. There, I use the yellowing seed heads of plume poppies and smoke bush to construct an arch that looked like it had been pulled from a meadow.

I doubt my readers will be moved to reproduce these floral fantasies; they would be difficult to throw together for a dinner party. But I hope these imaginings will inspire us all to recognize the essentialness of nature in both its wild and cultivated forms. As you wander the parks, forests, and fields that surround you, know that we, as flower-lovers, must protect and preserve uncultivated Mother Nature for future generations

FIT FOR A QUEEN

The wrought-iron bedsteads were so appealing in the turquoise bedroom
of this Mexican home that I clipped purple-blossomed vines from the
outdoor garden and invited them in. Known as *Petrea volubilis*, or queen's
wreath, this fast-growing vine seems a little like its northern cousin,
wisteria. Rather than keep them contained in this handsome compote,
I let the vines wander in their most natural form.

A smaller arrangement (see page 226) is repurposed here by adding it to a collection of five other vases holding a variety of bold-colored dahlias. They are arranged into an arch, complementing the chalk-pink walls. Once the event is over, an impression made, the vases can "travel" to other areas of the house and resume their individual status.

PROCEED WITH CAUTION

The Hudson River Valley, like much of the Northeast, has its share of
invasives. None is more frightening than Japanese knotweed, which can
grow unchecked and undermine whole foundations. A patch grew just
down the lane from this photographer's studio and, for this single two-
week period, its flowers were in bloom. Here was an opportunity to turn
a negative into a positive. I fashioned a chandelier (see page 231) out
of the fronds, an easy chore of securing the branches with floral wire.
Artemisia, another invasive, was also blooming nearby. I gathered branches
and secured them in long Pyrex dishes, where chicken wire pillows held
them upright to create an indoor meadow. The invasives in this unkempt
combination were quickly packaged and destroyed after the shoot.

A mauve tablecloth, napkins, and candles echo the woodwork, while pale lilac clematis graces the table.

My daughter, Celeste, and our Great Pyrenees mix Sky, pause in the afternoon light next to a compote of dahlias, lisianthuses, zinnias, foxgloves, and raspberry canes.

This bathtub fantasy invites the wild rose to invade this sky-blue bathroom. The full tub urges you to step in, but do tread carefully among the thorny vines.

CLIMBING THE STAIRS

With visions of an indoor meadow as inspiration, I combined Queen Anne's lace and northern sea oats to climb this winding staircase. How do you contain such numbers? Easy. Gather Pyrex baking dishes—the kind you use for making brownies—add chicken wire pillows secured with floral tape to the bottom, and add the foliage.

I designed this wrought-iron arch for wedding events; it contains vessels to hold water without using floral foam. Here, I added the seed heads of macleaya, or plume poppy, and smoke bush, as well as their foliage, to create an indoor celebration.

A gathering of 'Limelight' hydrangeas sea oats, and elderberry branches light up the olive walls of this faded manse. They join an arrangement of 'Queen Lime' zinnias on the marble table, evoking an era of plenty.

An orange-brown variety of heliopsis ('Bleeding Hearts') joins with
just-erupting milkweed pods to light up yellow fields of goldenrod.

ACKNOWLEDGMENTS

I am grateful to Leslie Jonath, who never gives up on me and is always there with the next bright idea.

To photographers Andrea Gentl and Martin Hyers, whose work takes my breath away and whose collaboration together is a beautiful dance to behold. Thank you also to photographers Gemma and Andy Ingalls, whose beautiful, important contributions are essential to this book.

Julie Michaels, who captures my voice and makes it better.

Emma Campion, my extraordinary art director, whose visions of beauty I am always ready to step into.

Dervla Kelly, my enthusiastic editor; Ashley Pierce, production editor; Mari Gill, production designer; Dan Myers, production manager, who put all of the pieces together.

Lydia Mongiardo, Georgene Poliak, and Yuko Yamamoto—your help, support, and love mean the world to me. Ella and Simone Long for bringing so much to the pink wonderland.

Sugar-flower wizard Marion Attal, who contributed the most delightful cake for this book. Kate Holt of the Ark Elements, who lent me such beautiful wares.

Thank you to homeowners Jennifer Murray and Patrick Stayer, Andrea Gentl and Martin Hyers, Frank Muytjens and Scott Edward Cole of the Inn at Kenmore Hall, Claudia Fernandez of Casa Puuc, John Powell and Josh Ramos of Urbano Rentals, Jade Snow Carroll and Ian Rausch, Stella DeLuca, Yuko Yamamoto and Ethan Palmer, Helen Dealtry and Dan Barry. What a gift to be able to photograph within your beautiful spaces.

The many wonderful growers whose flowers grace these pages: so much respect and admiration for the gifts you share with the world. Naomi Blumenthal, bearer of bounty, Diane Barrette of Renaissance Farm, Grace Lamb of Five Forks Farm, Anna Mac of Wild and Cultivated, Christa Stoziak of Markristo Farm, Marilyn Cederoth and Kate Swift of Cedar Farm, Gracielinda Poulson of Grace Rose Farm, Georgene Poliak of Maiden Flower Farm, and the folks at Bear Creek Farm.

And, finally, thank you to my beloved sister, Simone Chezar, for being the best sounding board; my father, Howard Chezar, for always believing in me; Chris Gregory, for his patience and support; my flower family, students and colleagues—the circle gets bigger every year: I love and admire you all so much. And thank you to my not-so-little children, August Oak and Celeste Neva, for keeping it real, and for letting me be your mama.

ABOUT THE CONTRIBUTORS

ARIELLA CHEZAR

Ariella is the author of *The Flower Workshop* and *Flowers for the Table* and a master floral designer who has appeared in numerous magazines, including *Oprah Daily*, *Martha Stewart Living*, and *Real Simple*. She is an instructor and artistic director at FlowerSchool New York, and has designed flower arrangements for the White House.

JULIE MICHAELS

Julie is an award-winning writer and editor with thirty years of experience in book publishing, newspaper, and magazine journalism. A former editor at the *Boston Globe*, Julie is co-author with Ariella Chezar of *The Flower Workshop* and *Seasonal Flower Arranging*, both published by Ten Speed Press. She lives and gardens in Western Massachusetts.

GENTL & HYERS

Andrea Gentl and Martin Hyers are the New York–based photography duo
Gentl and Hyers. The couple have photographed for multiple brands and editorial
and advertising clients. They are known for their work in still life, food, interiors,
beauty, and travel. In Spring 2022, Andrea Gentl wrote and photographed her
first cookbook, *Cooking With Mushrooms*, which won *Bon Appetit*'s Best Cookbook
of 2022.

THE INGALLS

The work of celebrated photographers Gemma and Andrew Ingalls of Ingalls
Photography has been featured in *Architectural Digest*, *New York Magazine*, and
Martha Stewart Living. They are based out of Brooklyn, New York.

Published in the United States by Ten Speed Press, an imprint of the Crown
Publishing Group, a division of Penguin Random House LLC, New York.
www.tenspeed.com

Ten Speed Press and the Ten Speed Press colophon are registered trademarks
of Penguin Random House LLC.

Typefaces: General Type's Cambon, Latinotype's Juana and Jazmin

Library of Congress Cataloging-in-Publication Data
Names: Chezar, Ariella, author. | Michaels, Julie, other. | Gentl & Hyers,
    photographer.
Title: Home in bloom : lessons for creating floral beauty in every room /
    Ariella Chezar with Julie Michaels ; photography by Gentl & Hyers.
Description: First edition. | California : Ten Speed Press, [2024] |
    Summary: "A vivid, inspiring look at the role of flowers and plants in
    interior design through the stunning, wild work of Ariella Chezar"--
    Provided by publisher.
Identifiers: LCCN 2023022095 (print) | LCCN 2023022096 (ebook) | ISBN
    9781984859099 (hardcover) | ISBN 9781984859105 (ebook)
Subjects: LCSH: Flower arrangement in interior decoration. | Floral
    decorations.
Classification: LCC SB449 .C4454 2024 (print) | LCC SB449 (ebook) | DDC
    745.92--dc23/eng/20230825
LC record available at https://lccn.loc.gov/2023022095
LC ebook record available at https://lccn.loc.gov/2023022096

Hardcover ISBN: 978-1-9848-5909-9
eBook ISBN: 978-1-9848-5910-5

Printed in China

Acquiring editor: Dervla Kelly | Production editor: Ashley Pierce
Designer: Emma Campion | Production designer: Mari Gill
Production manager: Dan Myers | Prepress color manager: Jane Chinn
Copyeditor: Alison Kerr Miller | Proofreader: Karen Thompson
Publicist: Erica Gelbard | Marketer: Brianne Sperber

10 9 8 7 6 5 4 3 2 1

First Edition